DEVELOPING LITERACY

Customisable teaching resources for literacy

GW00492943

WORD: STRUCTURE AND SPELLING

Ages 8–9

Christine Moorcroft

A & C Black • London

Contents

Spelling strategies

Published 2009 by A & C Black Publishers Limited
36 Soho Square, London W1D 3QY
www.acblack.com

ISBN 978-1-4081-0063-9

Copyright text © Christine Moorcroft 2009
Copyright illustrations © Sean Longcroft 2009
Copyright cover illustration © Piers Baker 2009
Editor: Dodi Beardshaw
Designed by Susan McIntyre

The authors and publishers would like to thank Ray Barker,
Collette Drifte and Rifat Siddiqui for their advice in producing this
series of books.

A CIP catalogue record for this book is available from the
British Library.

Printed and bound in Great Britain by Halstan Printing Group,
Amersham, Buckinghamshire.

A & C Black uses paper produced with elemental chlorine-free
pulp, harvested from managed sustainable forests.

Introduction

100% New Developing Literacy Word is a series of seven photocopiable activity books for developing children's ability to read fluently and automatically through using phonic knowledge of grapheme–phoneme correspondences and the skills of blending as their prime approach for decoding unfamiliar words. The series helps children to build up a store of words that they instantly recognise and understand on sight and to segment words into their constituent phonemes. It also helps them to develop skills in spelling words accurately by combining the use of grapheme–phoneme correspondence knowledge as the prime approach, and morphological knowledge and etymological information. They learn useful approaches for learning and spelling irregular words. The books contribute to the development of an understanding that spelling is the reverse of blending phonemes into words for reading. There are three books for children aged 4–7 (*Word: Recognition and Spelling*) and four books for children aged 7–11 (*Word: Structure and Spelling*).

100% New Developing Literacy Word: Structure and Spelling Ages 8–9 provides learning activities to support strand 6 (Word structure and spelling) of the literacy objectives of the Primary Framework for Literacy:

Strand 6 Word structure and spelling

- Use knowledge of phonics, morphology and etymology to spell new and unfamiliar words
- Distinguish the spelling and meaning of common homophones
- Know and apply common spelling rules
- Develop a range of personal strategies for learning new and irregular words

100% New Developing Literacy Word: Structure and Spelling Ages 8–9 provides support for teaching that develops from previous work based on the National Primary Strategy *Letters and Sounds: Principles and Practice of High Quality Phonics*.

The activities are arranged in three sections – Revision and consolidation, Spelling rules and Spelling strategies.

The activities

Some of activities can be carried out with the whole class; others are more suitable for small groups. Most of them are suitable for either collaborative or individual work, and can be particularly useful where the teacher and teaching assistants are working more closely with other groups. Some are generic and can be adapted, using the CD-ROM or masking when copying, for use with different words, graphemes or phonemes; the notes that follow and, in some cases, the notes at the foot of the page provide suggestions and ideas for this and for developing extension activities. Many of the activities can be adapted for use at different levels, to suit the differing levels of attainment of the children. Some can be used in different ways as explained in the notes.

Reading

Most children will be able to carry out the activities independently but a few will need help in reading the instructions on the sheets.

Organisation

The activities require very few resources besides pencils, crayons, scissors and dictionaries. Other materials are specified in the Teachers' notes on the pages: for example, interactive whiteboard, etymological dictionaries. Wherever appropriate, the children should be encouraged to check their answers using a dictionary.

Extension activities

Most of the activity sheets end with a challenge (*Now try this!*) which reinforces and extends the children's learning. These more challenging activities might be appropriate for only a few children; it is not expected that the whole class should complete them, although many more children might benefit from them with appropriate assistance – possibly as a guided or shared activity. On some pages there is space for the children to complete the extension activities, but others will require a notebook or a separate sheet of paper.

Accompanying CD

The enclosed CD-ROM contains all the activity sheets from the book and allows you to edit them for printing or saving. This means that modifications can be made to differentiate the activities further to suit individual pupils' needs. See page 12 for more details.

Notes on the activities

The notes which follow expand upon those which are provided at the bottom of most activity pages. They give ideas and suggestions for making the most of the activity sheet, including suggestions for the whole-class introduction, the plenary session or for follow-up work using an adapted version of the activity sheet.

Terms and abbreviations used

Base word
A word which might stand on its own as a meaningful word and to which suffixes and prefixes can be added to form other related words.

Digraph
A two-letter grapheme in which the two letters represent one sound ('two letters – one sound'): for example, **ck** in *back*, **oo** in *boot*, and **ch** in *chain*.

Grapheme
A symbol that represents a phoneme. The symbol can consist of one or more letters: for example, **b**, **a**, **ai**, **igh**, **eigh**, **sh**, **tch**. The 26 letters of the English alphabet are combined in various ways to form the graphemes necessary to represent the phonemes of spoken English. For a complete list, see *Letters and Sounds* pages 25–27.

Morpheme
The smallest morphological unit of language, which cannot be analysed into smaller units.

Morphology
The form (including change, formation and inflection) of words in a language.

Phoneme
The smallest unit of sound in a word that can change its meaning: for example, in the words *lad* and *lid* the difference between the phonemes /**a**/ and /**i**/ creates the difference in meaning between the words. Most linguists agree that spoken English uses about 44 phonemes: for a complete list, see *Letters and Sounds*, pages 23–24.

Phonics
Skills of segmenting and blending sounds within words and an understanding of how to use the phonic 'code' of English in reading and spelling.

Segment
A meaningful section of a word, which might be a prefix or suffix or another section: for example, *flect* in *deflect*, *reflect*.

Split digraph
A digraph with a letter that splits (comes between) the two letters in the digraph: for example, in *bite* and *tide*, the **d** splits the digraph *ie*, which represents the phoneme /**i**/.

To segment
To break down words into their constituent phonemes in order to spell them.

Trigraph
A three-letter grapheme in which the three letters represent one sound ('three letters – one sound'): for example, **eau** in *bureau* and **igh** in *right*. There are also four-letter graphemes: for example, **eigh** to represent the /**ai**/ phoneme in *neigh*.

Revision and consolidation

The activities in this section help to consolidate the children's learning from last year about how prefixes and suffixes alter the meaning of a base word and how the spellings of base words change when these affixes are used. The activities build upon this to develop the children's understanding of the ways in which suffixes can form a different class of word (verb, noun, adjective, adverb). There is also consolidation of contractions, less common grapheme–phoneme correspondences, common, similar-sounding, word endings and commonly misspelled words containing double consonants.

Know your ions (page 13) helps to consolidate the children's knowledge of the use of the suffixes -**tion** and -**sion**: how they form a noun from another word and how they affect the spelling of the base word. They use morphology to spell new words. You could help them to look for rules for adding -**tion** or -**sion** (and how to tell when this should become -**ssion**; see below). For example, words ending with -**de** usually take -**sion**: *collide/collision, corrode/corrosion, divide/division, invade/invasion, persuade/persuasion*; words ending with -**scribe** change this to -**script**: *describe/description, inscribe/inscription, prescribe/ prescription, subscribe/subscription*. However some words ending with a vowel and then **t** take -**tion** (*exhibit/exhibition, inhibit/ inhibition, prohibit/prohibition*), while others change the **t** to **s** and take -**sion**: *admit/admission, submit/submission, transmit/transmission*. Some children could explore these words and come up with a rule (words ending vowel, consonant, vowel, consonant take -**tion** while those ending consonant, consonant, vowel, consonant change the final **t** to **s** and take -**sion**). Encourage the children to explore other -**ion** words: for example, those formed from base words ending -**ode** (*corrode/corrosion, erode/erosion*), also -**ose** (*compose/composition, expose/ exposition, propose/proposition*). They could enter their findings in a table using a spreadsheet. Encourage them to look for similarities and then when they find an exception, to look for other words similar to this exception.

Noun maker (page 14) consolidates the children's knowledge of the use of the suffixes -**ment** and -**ness** to form nouns from verbs or adjectives. You could model how to choose between the endings in cases where the children are not sure by 'thinking aloud': *Holyment... no, that isn't a real word... Holiness... yes, I've heard that word before.* The children should complete the page before using a dictionary to check their answers. To develop their understanding of the different types of words you could help them to use them in sentences: *I agree with you. We have an agreement; Can you enlarge this picture? Can you make an enlargement of this picture?* Ask the children to write their own sentences using two -**ment** and two -**ness** words.

Plural sort (page 15) helps to consolidate the children's knowledge of the suffixes for creating plurals. Some children might find it helpful to write the plural for each word on another piece of paper first, and then decide which rule it uses before writing each word on a notepad on the sheet. They use spelling rules for forming plurals: for most words, add **s**; for words ending -**ch**, -**s**, -**sh**, -**ss**, -**z** or -**zz** add -**es**; for words ending with a consonant then **y**, change the **y** to **i** and add -**es**: for most words ending with **f**, change the **f** to **v** and add -**es** (exceptions are *briefs, chiefs, dwarfs or dwarves, hoofs or hooves, roofs*); most words ending with **o** just take **s**, but a few take -**es** (*cargoes, haloes, heroes, echoes, potatoes, tomatoes*); irregular plurals, such as *children, mice* and *women*, have to be learned. Answers: *activities, addresses, anniversaries, computers, countries, elves, fifties, flexes, halves, harnesses, headaches, leaves, pianos, puzzles, Saturdays, secretaries, shelves, shoeboxes, stitches, wolves; feet, geese, teeth.*

Short change (page 16) focuses on common spelling rules. It helps to consolidate the children's knowledge of contractions of common words: two words are combined and one or more letters are missed out and replaced with an apostrophe. The children should have had previous experience of contracting words by combining two words and using an apostrophe to mark where letters are omitted. Here they have practice in proofreading, identifying and correcting mistakes. It is useful to remind them that an apostrophe is never used for making a plural, unless it indicates ownership: for example, *the children's lunchboxes, the family's address, the Jacksons' house.*

Ending in -le, -el, -al or -il (page 17) consolidates the children's knowledge of alternative graphemes for the 'el' sound at the end of a word. It also helps to develop strategies for learning new words. To help them to remember these endings, encourage them to use 'spellspeak' (enunciating the words in a way that makes the unstressed vowel clear: for example, *caram-ell, chan-ell, cyc-luh, ger-bill*). This is a useful strategy where spelling rules are difficult to apply: for example, *lentil/gentle, table/label.* However, it is worth noting that most words ending -**ical** are adjectives: this makes spelling rules easier to apply to *comical/cubicle.*

Rogue words (page 18) consolidates and develops phonics skills by focusing on the knowledge of a less common grapheme for the /**g**/ phoneme. You might need to introduce, or remind the children of crossword conventions: for example how the clues are numbered down and across. Other useful words include *analogue, brogue, colleague, guild, guilt, guilty, guitar, intrigue, meringue, monologue, prologue, vogue.*

Here is the completed crossword:

	c¹								d²		l³
	a		d⁴	i	s	g	u	i	s	e	
	t	g⁵					a		a		
b⁶	a	g	u	e	t⁷	t	e		l	g	
	l	e		o			l		o	u	
	o	s⁸	y	n	a	g	o	g	u	e	
	g	s		g			u				
	u			u		g⁹	u	e	s	t	
	e			e		u					
				v¹⁰	a	g	u	e			
						r					
f¹¹	a	t	i	g	u	e	d				

Prefix opposites (page 19) develops a knowledge of morphology and spelling rules: it consolidates the children's knowledge of prefixes that can form opposites. If the children are unsure, they should try out different prefixes orally until they come to one that they have heard before or that sounds right. Spelling rules to consider are: words beginning **b** or **p** usually take **im-**; words beginning **l** usually take **il-**; words beginning **r** usually take **ir-**, depending on the meanings created.

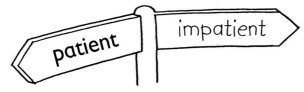

Spelling choice (page 20) consolidates and develops phonics skills by focusing on the knowledge of the different graphemes for the /ə/ phoneme at the end of a word. Remind the children that most words for people doing an action end with **-er**, although some end **-re** or **-or** (*neighbour* is unusual but is not a word for someone doing an action). Abstract nouns tend to end with **-our** (*behaviour, colour, favour, flavour, glamour, labour, rumour, splendour*). Other useful words include *cleaner, employer, listener, player, prisoner, smuggler; centre, fibre, litre, massacre, metre* (and other metric measures), *ogre; beggar, binoculars, calendar, circular, dollar, familiar, muscular, popular, spectacular.* The children could collect examples of words ending with the /ə/ phoneme and record them in columns in a table using a word processor.

Double or single (page 21) consolidates the children's knowledge of spelling rules by providing practice in choosing either a single or double consonant to fill a gap in a word and how a single or double consonant can change a vowel phoneme. In many cases this can be figured out by considering pronunciation: for example, *bonnet* (/**o**/), rather then *bonet* (/**ow**/); *silent* (/**igh**/ rather than *sillent* (/**i**/); *tuna* (/**oo**/), rather than *tunna* (/**u**/). However, this rule does not always apply (*camera, capital, lily, popular*). You could set the children challenges to find words with double and single consonants that follow the rules and those that do not. Also play a game in which you say a word and the children hold up a card saying 'double' if it contains a double consonant. Choose one holding up a card and ask him or her which consonant is doubled.

Spelling rules

The activities in this section concentrate on knowledge of phonics (phoneme–grapheme correspondences), morphology (the formation of words: adding prefixes or suffixes to base words and the understanding of how suffixes can convert a word into a word of a different class – noun/verb/adjective/adverb).

All of an age (page 22) is about using knowledge of morphology (converting verbs to nouns) and applying common spelling rules (changing the spellings of base words, where necessary, before adding a suffix beginning with a vowel). Highlighting the use of spelling rules for changing the spelling of the base word will help the children to spell difficult words such as *marriage* and *carriage*. Through completing sentences the children learn the ways in which the linked words can be used as mnemonics as well as how to adapt the spelling of a base word before adding a suffix. Start by reading the sentences in the first example with the children and ask them what each one tells them, pointing out that they give the same information using different forms of the main word.

What's my line? (page 23) focuses on common spelling rules: adapting the spelling of a base word before adding **-ist**. It also develops knowledge of morphology: the children learn that words ending **-ist** are generally words for people doing an action or job. Note that many of them apply to music, other arts or science. Other useful words include *chemist, dentist* (Latin *dens* – tooth), *florist* (Latin *flos* – flower), *oboist, organist, palmist, specialist.* Ask the children to write three rules for adding **-ist** to a word to make a noun for a person.

Word factory and **Glossary** (pages 24–25) develop knowledge of morphology and common spelling rules and there are also opportunities to develop knowledge of etymology. Note that words ending -**ary** are usually nouns for places in which items are kept, whereas -**ory** words are mainly for places in which a specific activity is carried out (including *memory* – where remembering takes place) or where people live, and that the meanings of the base words are not always recognisable because they come from Latin. Other useful words, which have retained the Latin -**orium** ending: *auditorium, crematorium, sanatorium*. Some -**ary** nouns are not the names of places (*anniversary, burglary, centenary, commentary, confectionary, constabulary, documentary*). There are also -**ary** adjectives: *contemporary, culinary, customary, exemplary, hereditary, imaginary, ordinary, stationary*. In **Glossary**, there are both Latin and Greek words: *diarius* (daily), *mortuus* (dead), *glossa* (explanation), *dictio* (word, phrase), *pharmakon* (drug), *liber* (book), *avis* (bird).

Community of words (page 26) develops knowledge of morphology and common spelling rules. The children should recognise that the words in bold type do not sound right in the sentences and they should now be developing skills in adding suffixes to change words from one class to another. After they have completed the activity it is useful to invite feedback and to discuss why some words can just have -**ty** added, whereas others need to be changed: ask them to try saying *publicty, agilety, ablety* and so on, and point out how and why the ending is changed. These words would sound clumsy. The children could also write some rules for adding -**ty**. Note that most words ending vowel, consonant, **e** lose the **e** and add **i** before -**ty** is added, but that *safety* does not. They could collect other examples of -**ty** words and compare the ways in which the endings of the root words change. Other useful words include: *eternal/eternity, immune/immunity, mature/maturity, obese/obesity, rare/rarity, secure/security, senior/seniority, stable/stability, stupid/stupidity*. Note the changes in some vowel phonemes and changes in stress: for example, *clear/clarity, fatal/fatality, national/nationality, original/originality, sane/sanity*. Also note changed endings of base words in *humble/humility, poor/poverty*.

Word dance and **Making a difference** (pages 27–28) are concerned with developing knowledge of morphology and common spelling rules. These activities focus on forming nouns. Ask the children to notice which root words change before -**ance** is added, and how; they should consider words ending with **e**, **er** and **y**. Also discuss the ways in which words change before -**ence** is added: words ending -**end** and -**e**, also the few ending -**ey** (*disobey, obey*). Also note any changes in phonemes when -**ence** is added: for example, *confer/conference, obey/obedience, subside/subsidence, refer/reference, reside/residence*. The children could collect

other examples for comparison or you could use the CD-ROM to adapt page 27: *admit/admittance, appear/appearance, assist/assistance, attend/attendance, defy/defiance, inherit/inheritance, insure/insurance, perform/performance, rely/reliance, resist/resistance, tolerate/tolerance*. Ask the children to write sentences using four of the -**ance** nouns.

Selective adjectives, **Adjective arithmetic**, **That's fantastic!** and **Special adjectives** (pages 29–32) develop knowledge of morphology and common spelling rules. They focus on common endings for adjectives, and the children learn to recognise these endings and how the spellings of the base words change when they are added. Some children might find it helpful to write out the words with their -**ive** endings on a separate piece of paper first, and then allocate them to groups on the sheet. **Selective adjectives** focuses on classifying the adjectives according to how the base words change when -**ive** is added to verbs. **Adjective arithmetic** deals with forming adjectives from nouns by adding -**ous**. **That's fantastic!** challenges the children to proofread a text, identify words that should be adjectives and correct them by adding the ending -**ic** to nouns. To support lower-attaining children, you could highlight some of the wrong words in the passage before giving them the sheet. **Special adjectives** asks the children to form adjectives to match descriptive phrases by adding -**ial** to a word in the phrases. You could use the interactive whiteboard to display the appropriate types of words that can be made into adjectives with each ending and ask the children to add the suffix. They can then use the spellchecker to check their answers.

Hidden a and double ll (page 33) focuses on developing knowledge of morphology and common spelling rules. Remind the children of the suffix -**ly** and ask them to use words ending **ly** to describe actions that you do: for example, walking (quickly or slowly), writing (neatly, tidily, untidily). The activity deals with a common ending for adverbs (-**ly**) when added to adjectives ending -**al**, in which there is usually an unstressed **a** and double **l**, since the base word remains unchanged when -**ly** is added. This page can be adapted using the CD-ROM: *casual/casually, commercial/commercially, critical/critically, electrical/electrically, exceptional/exceptionally, experimental/experimentally, financial/financially, gradual/gradually, historical/historically, horizontal/horizontally, ideal/ideally, logic/logically,*

practical/practically. Note that the syllable containing the /**a**/ phoneme is often omitted in speech but that even where this syllable is enunciated no /**a**/ phoneme is heard; it sounds more like **ə** ('uh').

To double or not to double (page 34) develops knowledge of morphology and common spelling rules. Write up some present tense verbs and ask the children to use a suffix to make them into the past tense: for example, *hurry, jump, stop*. Discuss rules for changing the base word. In this activity, the children decide which verbs ending **l** double the **l** when the past tense ending **-ed** is added. It builds on the children's previous learning about past tense endings and their effects on base words. You could help them to formulate rules for keeping single **l** or doubling the **l**. Words with a single vowel before the final **l** usually double the **l** but those with two vowels usually retain a single **l**. After completing the page the children could check their answers using a dictionary or spell checker and then draw up rules for doubling **l**. The children will notice that *dialled* and *fuelled* have double **ll**, whereas in most words where **l** follows two vowels it is not doubled. Ask them to say the word aloud and to say what they notice about the sounds of the **u** and **e** (they are pronounced as two separate phonemes, although not always very distinctly). Examples of other words that change in similar ways before a suffix is added are *duell/duelling*, *trial/trialled* (but *trail/trailed*, because the **ai** grapheme represents a single phoneme).

Verbifying and **Verb brain** (pages 35–36) are about morphology and common spelling rules. The children learn two common verb endings and form verbs from nouns and adjectives, using what they know about changes to base word endings. These pages can be adapted using the CD-ROM: *class/classify, dignity/dignify, intense/intensify, mummy/mummify, note/notify, solid/solidify; advise, baptise, centralise, commercialise, computerise, harmonise, modernise, motorise, publicise.*

Vowel change (page 37) focuses on morphology and common spelling rules with a special emphasis on verbs in which a medial vowel phoneme changes when the ending **-en** is added to the base word. Some verbs that end with a long /**igh**/ vowel phoneme represented by a split digraph **i-e** change to a short vowel by doubling the consonant **t** or **d** before **-en** is added: for example, *bite/bitten, drive/driven, hide/hidden, ride/ridden, write/written*. Some verbs change medial vowel phoneme /**ee**/ (spelt **ea** or **ee**) to /**ow**/ (spelt **o**) before **-en** is added: *freeze/frozen, steal/stolen, speak/spoken, weave/woven* (there

are other, less common ones, such as *cleave/cloven*). Some verbs change medial vowel phoneme /**e**/ (spelt **ea**) to /**o**/ before **-en** is added: *tread/trodden*. Some verbs change medial vowel phoneme /**oo**/ to /**ow**/ (spelt **o**) before **-en** is added: *choose/chosen*. There is no rule for recognising when a verb will change in this way. They need to be learned.

Spot the mistake ee (page 38) helps the children to learn common spelling rules. It consolidates their previous learning of alternative graphemes for the /**ee**/ phoneme and draws on their growing knowledge of words. Read some or all of the words aloud to the children before they see this page. Ask them how they are similar: they all contain the /**ee**/ phoneme. Ask volunteers to write the letters that can be used to spell this phoneme. Using the CD-ROM, this page could be adapted for focusing on the graphemes used for spelling any commonly misspelled phoneme.

Not the ay phoneme (page 39) helps the children to learn common spelling rules. It consolidates their previous learning of the **ai** grapheme and draws on their growing vocabulary of words they can read on sight. Compare these with the words on page 23 to help the children to avoid confusing **-ian** and **ain** endings and remind them that **-ian** usually indicates a person's job.

Mobile phone spellings 2 U, **Mobile phone spellings 4 u** and **Gr8 mobile phone spellings** (pages 40–42) help the children to learn common spelling rules. For **Mobile phone spellings 4 u** ask children to use mobile phones to spell some words using the number 2 to replace letters that sound like 2: *to, today, tomorrow, tonight, too, tooth*. For **Mobile phone spellings 4 u** ask children to use mobile phones to spell some words using the number 4 to replace letters that sound like 4: *fall, for, form, fortune, forward*. For **Gr8 mobile phone spellings** ask children to use mobile phones to spell some words using the number 8 to replace letters that sound like 8: *great, plate, skate, straight, weight*. These activities consolidate their previous learning of alternative graphemes for the /**oo**/, /**or**/ and /**ai**/ phonemes and draw on their growing vocabulary of words they can read on sight. The children could also write and 'translate' mobile phone messages that use all of these numbers plus a range of other mobile phone abbreviations.

Number plate spellings (page 43) develops knowledge of common spelling rules. It features vowel phonemes that can be spelled in various ways. You could also challenge the children to note down staff car number plates and try to create words by adding letters to them. Ask the children to think about the different ways of spelling the missing phonemes and, if necessary, to try them out on a separate piece of paper and to choose the one that looks correct.

Homophone hints (page 44) is about distinguishing the spellings and meanings of common homophones. Ask the children to think about the different ways of spelling each phoneme and to consider the type and meaning of word: for example, *allowed* has a past tense -**ed** suffix and means *let*. The children should use their knowledge of other, linked words to help them and should draw on their knowledge of past tense suffixes, comparative adjective suffixes, irregular past tenses and **al/le** endings. You could use the CD-ROM to edit the activity, providing clues for other pairs of homophones: *bare/bear, beach/beech, beat/beet, board/bored, brake/break, brews/bruise, by/bye/buy, caught/court, cell/sell, cent/scent/sent, coarse/course, crews/cruise, currant/current, ewe/yew/you, fair/fare, fate/fete, flea/flee, flour/flower, grate/great, groan/grown, guessed/guest, hale/hail, hare/hair, hear/here, heard/herd, higher/hire, idle/idol, knew/new, larva/lava, leak/leek, made/maid, mail/male, maize/maze, mare/mayor, medal/meddle, missed/mist, moor/more, night/knight, pain/pane, pause/paws/pores/pours, pear/pair, peace/piece, plane/plain, pore/pour/poor, rain/rein/reign, raise/raze/rays, road/rode/rowed, scene/seen, sew/so/sow, sight/site, soar/sore/saw, stake/steak, stalk/stork, stares/stairs, steal/steel, they're/their/there, throne/thrown, vain/vane/vein, waist/waste, wait/weight, whale/wail, war/wore, week/weak, were/where/wear, whether/weather, which/witch, would/wood, write/right, yoke/yolk.*

There is a high mountain nearby.

Spelling strategies

In this section there are activities that develop the children's knowledge about the roots of words and how words are constructed from meaningful segments, including prefixes and suffixes. There are activities to develop a range of strategies to help the children to read and spell unfamiliar or difficult words using analogy and mnemonics and 'spellspeak' to remember unstressed vowels and unpronounced letters.

In and out, **Up and down** and **Under or over** (pages 45–47) develop knowledge of morphology, focusing on the meanings of the prefixes and the ways in which they change the meanings of the base words. It is useful to mention to children that new words and usages can emerge.

Word-bites, **Word-core** and **Word petals** (pages 48–50) develop the children's knowledge of etymology, thus equipping them to develop personal strategies for learning new words. **Word-bites** focuses on words formed from commonly-used

word segments that come from Latin or Greek. **Word-core** presents a single word segment (*spect*) that occurs in many English words but comes from Latin *spicere* (to look). The children could work in small groups to discuss the connection between all the words and, during the plenary session, present their ideas to the class. **Word petals** presents the Greek suffix -**logy** (study), along with word segments from Greek and Latin which can precede it in English words. The children should match the clues to the definitions and create -**logy** words.

Compound pairs (page 51) develops the children's knowledge of phonics and morphology, with a focus on the different words that can be formed from the same main word. To illustrate the usefulness of knowing about compound words as a spelling strategy, you could read aloud a sentence, and ask the children to suggest how to spell a target word, e.g. *'We need a watertight container.'* The children could discuss splitting *watertight* into two recognisable words.

Prefix it and **Number prefixes** (pages 52–53) develop the children's knowledge of morphology and etymology. Here they learn about segments of words, which are not complete English words in themselves, unlike the separate words that make up compound words. The segments on page 52 are derived from their roots in other languages, particularly Latin: *hale* (*inhale, exhale*) – *halare* (*breathe*); *port* (*import, export*) – *portare* (*carry*); *scend* (*ascend, descend*) – *scandere* (*climb*); *struct* (*constructive, destructive*) – *struct* (from *struere* – *build*); *flate* (*inflate, deflate*) – *flare* (*blow*); *clude* (*include, exclude*) – *claudere* (*shut, closed*). The children might be able to find other words that contain these segments. Tell them that number prefixes come from the Latin and Greek words for the numbers.

Word spiders, **A base to build on** and **Word changer** (pages 54–56) develop the children's knowledge of morphology and etymology as they build words from segments which should be becoming increasingly familiar. All three activities can be edited using the CD-ROM for practice with other word segments. For **Word changer**, the teacher could read a sequence of the words aloud and ask children to attempt to spell them, then discuss their attempts with a partner.

A chewy problem and **In the queue** (pages 57–58) develop the children's knowledge of morphology and common spelling rules. Knowledge of the **tu** and **cu** graphemes for the *chew* and *queue* blends of phonemes in words becomes part of their spelling knowledge and helps to increase the range of words they can spell automatically.

Word segments (page 59) focus on common spelling rules linked with etymology and morphology. The children use word segments that come from a range of sources and use their knowledge of spelling rules to modify base words when adding suffixes. They will have learned how to split words into syllables – you could remind them of this previous work and then tell them that some words can be split into segments that have meanings but which might contain more than one syllable, for example *over*, *under*, *photo*.

Help words (page 60) helps the children to use their knowledge of morphology and etymology to spell new and unfamiliar words and encourages them to develop personal strategies for learning new and irregular words. It assists with reading and spelling unfamiliar words containing less common alternative graphemes through introducing a strategy to help – the use of mnemonics. The children should notice that the 'help words' contain the tricky grapheme that is in the other words but with the unpronounced letter being pronounced.

Help sentences (page 61) develops the children's range of strategies for spelling tricky words containing less common phoneme–grapheme correspondences through the use of mnemonics. Encourage them to make up their own 'help sentences' for words they find difficult, especially those containing letters which are not pronounced, and to share these during plenary sessions.

Word stories and **New words** (pages 62–63) encourage the children to use their knowledge of morphology and etymology to spell new and unfamiliar words and encourage them to develop personal strategies for learning new and irregular words. You could ask the children to research a word and to prepare a short presentation to the class to explain how its irregular spelling came about, including the language it came from. Encourage them to use the interactive whiteboard to aid their presentation, which could include drawings, photographs and sound.

Great ideas (page 64) encourages the children to develop and share personal strategies for learning new and irregular words. They could also make a display of 'great ideas' in which they draw and cut out larger light bulbs to fix onto a display board, to show how they remember the spellings of words they have trouble with. Alternatively, the display could be produced on a computer – you could even make the 'loght bulbs' flash on and off.

Using the CD-ROM

The CD-ROM included with this book contains an easy-to-use software program that allows you to print out pages from the book, to view them (e.g. on an interactive whiteboard) or to customise the activities to suit the needs of your pupils.

Getting started

It's easy to run the software. Simply insert the CD-ROM into your CD drive and the disk should autorun and launch the interface in your web browser.

If the disk does not autorun, open 'My Computer' and select the CD drive, then open the file 'start.html'.

Please note: this CD-ROM is designed for use on a PC. It will also run on most Apple Macintosh computers in Safari however, due to the differences between Mac and PC fonts, you may experience some unavoidable variations in the typography and page layouts of the activity sheets.

The Menu screen

Four options are available to you from the main menu screen.

The first option takes you to the Activity Sheets screen, where you can choose an activity sheet to edit or print out using Microsoft Word.

(If you do not have the Microsoft Office suite, you might like to consider using OpenOffice instead. This is a multi-platform and multi-lingual office suite, and an 'open-source' project. It is compatible with all other major office suites, and the product is free to download, use and distribute. The homepage for OpenOffice on the Internet is: www.openoffice.org.)

The second option on the main menu screen opens a PDF file of the entire book using Adobe Reader (see below). This format is ideal for printing out copies of the activity sheets or for displaying them, for example on an interactive whiteboard.

The third option allows you to choose a page to edit from a text-only list of the activity sheets, as an alternative to the graphical interface on the Activity Sheets screen.

Adobe Reader is free to download and to use. If it is not already installed on your computer, the fourth link takes you to the download page on the Adobe website.

You can also navigate directly to any of the three screens at any time by using the tabs at the top.

The Activity Sheets screen

This screen shows thumbnails of all the activity sheets in the book. Rolling the mouse over a thumbnail highlights the page number and also brings up a preview image of the page.

Click on the thumbnail to open a version of the page in Microsoft Word (or an equivalent software program, see above.) The full range of editing tools are available to you here to customise the page to suit the needs of your particular pupils. You can print out copies of the page or save a copy of your edited version onto your computer.

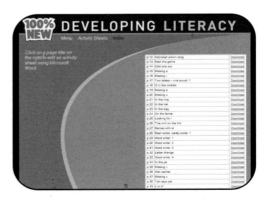

The Index screen

This is a text-only version of the Activity Sheets screen described above. Choose an activity sheet and click on the 'download' link to open a version of the page in Microsoft Word to edit or print out.

Technical support

If you have any questions regarding the *100% New Developing Literacy* or *Developing Mathematics* software, please email us at the address below. We will get back to you as quickly as possible.

educationalsales@acblack.com

Know your ion s

- **Make a word ending** sion **or** tion **from the word in bold type.**
- **Write it in the box.**
- **Read the sentence with the new word.**

We asked for **permit**

permission

to go to the shops.

We gave the police officer a **describe** of the burglar.

Our school is going to have an **inspect** today.

I know the **solve** to the problem.

In the fifth century there was an **invade** of Vikings.

We paid a £3 **admit** charge to go to the festival.

We saw an **exhibit** of sculpture at the art gallery.

I have a new **construct** set that has wheels, cogs and axles.

NOW TRY THIS!

- **Use what you know about** ion **endings to make** ion **words from these base words.**

declare   subscribe   submit

congratulate   persuade

Teachers' note Read the first example aloud with the children (using the word in bold type – *permit*) and ask them if the sentence sounds right. Ask what is wrong with it and re-read the sentence using *permission* instead of *permit*. Focus on the -**sion** ending and the change made to the base word (**t** is taken off and **s** is added – in addition to the **s** of -**sion**).

100% New Developing Literacy
Word: Structure and Spelling
Ages 8–9
© A & C BLACK

13

Noun maker

• Play Noun maker.

★ You need a partner, a dice and two counters.

★ Cut out the cards and shuffle them. Place your counters at Start.

★ Take turns to roll the dice and move that number of places. If you land on a base word, pick a card. If you can make a new word from the base word and the card, write the new word and keep the card. If you can't, return the card to the pack.

★ The winner is the player with the most new words when all the cards have been used.

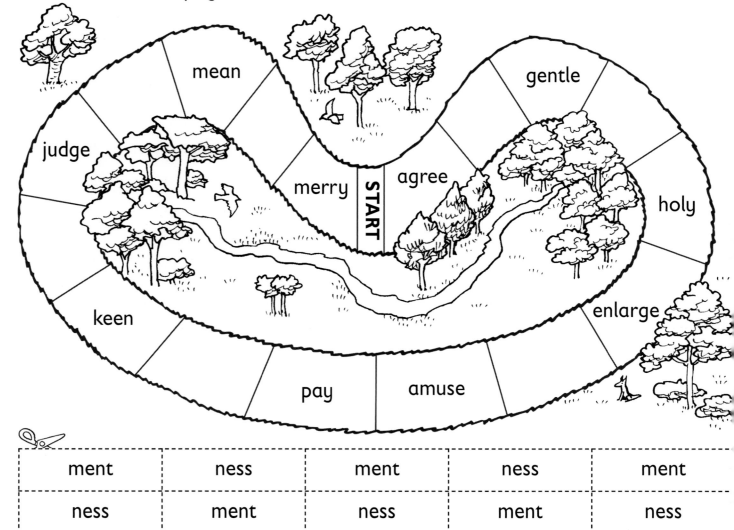

ment	ness	ment	ness	ment
ness	ment	ness	ment	ness

NOW TRY THIS!

• **Write sentences using two** ⬛ ment ⬛ **words and two** ⬛ ness ⬛ **words.**

Teachers' note The children will have formed words using the suffixes **-ness** and **-ment** but might not be aware that these words are nouns. Practise recognising abstract nouns (although this term need not be introduced) by using them in sentences and identifying words that need **-ment** or **-ness** to make sense.

100% New Developing Literacy
Word: Structure and Spelling
Ages 8–9
© A & C BLACK

Plural sort

- **Write the plural of each noun on a notepad.**
- **Write captions about the rules.**

activity   elf   headache   secretary
address   fifty   leaf   shelf
anniversary   flex   piano   shoebox
computer   half   puzzle   stitch
country   harness   Saturday   wolf

Write the plurals with others that follow the same rule.

One has been done for you.

computers

Just add 's'.

NOW TRY THIS!

- **Write the plurals for these words.**
- **Write the rule they follow.**

      foot   goose   tooth

Teachers' note Provide examples of simple plurals to remind the children how they are formed by adding the suffix **-s** or **-es**. Draw attention to any changes to the spelling of the noun when the suffix is added. See *Notes on the activities* page 6 for some useful spelling rules.

**100% New Developing Literacy
Word: Structure and Spelling
Ages 8–9
© A & C BLACK**

15

Short change

- **Proofread the letter.**
- **Cross out the wrong contractions.**
- **Write them correctly in the margin.**

	6 Do'nt Go Street
I'm	Parkside
	PAR2 6SE
	Wednesday 6th June
	Dear Rashid
	I'm typing this on my laptop on the train. Were going to go to London to stay with my Auntie May. Sh'es my dad's sister. Ill see my cousins Lydia and Jake.
	Mum said shed take us to the Natural History Museum. Its great there. Theyv'e got dinosaur skeletons and all kinds of fossils. Weve been there a few times but I never get bored with it. I think y'oud like it.
	Before we go there Mums taking us shopping. Shell spend hours in big shops trying on clothes. Then well have to help her to carry all the bags. I cant complain though, because theres fun to come afterwards.
	I hope your having a good holiday and youll come and see us when we get back. That's all for now.
	From Sarah

NOW TRY THIS!

- **Use these contractions in full sentences.**

  they'd   you've   who's   it's   here's   shouldn't

Teachers' note Help the children to identify the mistakes by 'thinking aloud': read the first line of the address with the children: *6 Do'nt Go Street – Do'nt* looks strange. There is no letter missing where the apostrophe is. *Don't* means do not, *so the apostrophe should go where the second o is missed out.*

100% New Developing Literacy Word: Structure and Spelling Ages 8–9
© A & C BLACK

Ending in [le], [el], [al] or [il]

Complete the words with [le], [el], [al], or [il].
Write them in the list that they match.

Use a dictionary.

caram____   cyc____   fin____   jew____   pup____
chann____   dazz____   foss____   lent____   stenc____
comic____   examp____   funer____   lev____   vit____
cubic____   festiv____   grumb____   nostr____   weas____

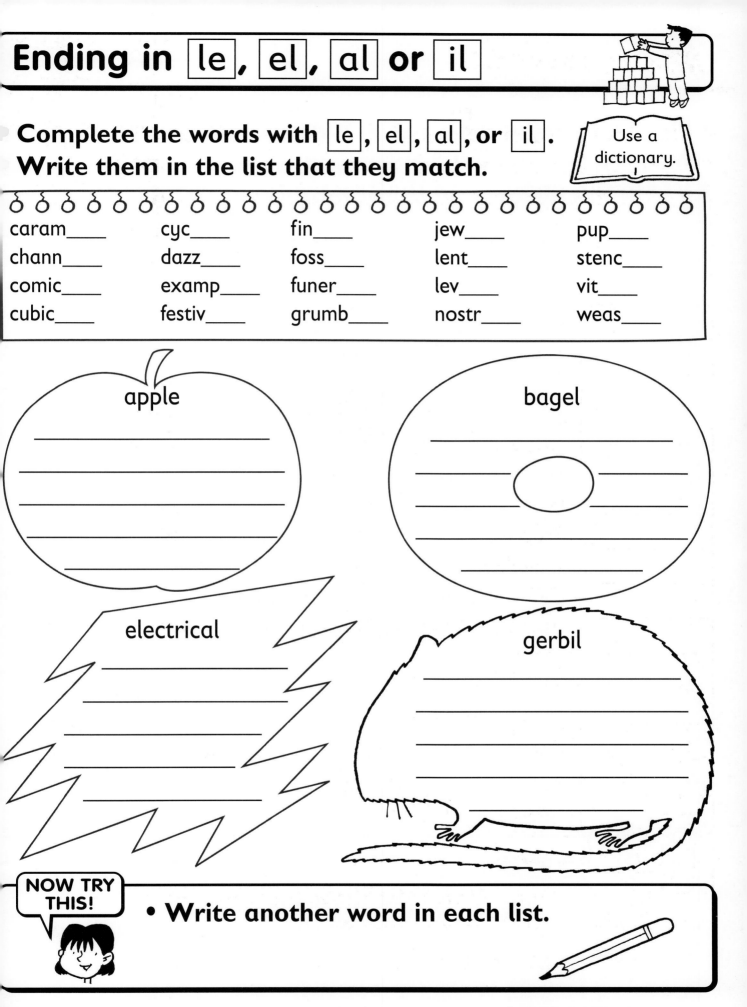

apple

bagel

electrical

gerbil

NOW TRY THIS!

• **Write another word in each list.**

Teachers' note The children should have had previous experience of reading and writing words with all these endings. Point them out in any shared texts and help them to remember them by saying the words as they are spelled, with an emphasis on the last syllable: for example, pup-**ill**, dazz-**luh**, caram-**ell**, festiv-**al**.

100% New Developing Literacy
Word: Structure and Spelling
Ages 8–9
© A & C BLACK

Rogue words

- **Match the definitions to the words with the** [g] **phoneme spelled** [gu].
- **Write the answers on the crossword.**

Clues

Across

4 Something worn to hide your identity (8)
6 Long French loaf (8)
8 Jewish place of worship (9)
9 A visitor invited to your home (5)
10 Not clear (5)
11 Tired (8)

Use a dictionary.

Answers

baguette
catalogue
dialogue
disguise
fatigued
guard
guess
guest
league
synagogue
tongue
vague

Down

1 A brochure of goods for sale (9)
2 Conversation (8)
3 Football teams play in a group called a ____ (6)
5 Answer given when you don't know (5)
7 You taste with it (6)
9 Keep safe (5)

NOW TRY THIS!

- **Write a word beginning** [gu] **that means to show the way. It can also mean a person who shows the way.**
- **Write this word in two different sentences.**

Teachers' note Remind the children that **gu** represents the phoneme /g/ and read the answers with them. They then have the task of matching the answers to the clues. This should not be guesswork. The use of a dictionary is recommended.

100% New Developing Literacy
Word: Structure and Spelling
Ages 8–9
© A & C BLACK

Prefix opposites

- **Choose a prefix to make a word with the opposite meaning.**
- **Write the new word on the sign.**

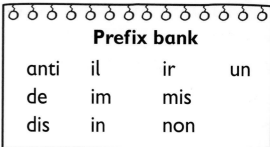

Prefix bank

anti	il	ir	un
de	im	mis	
dis	in	non	

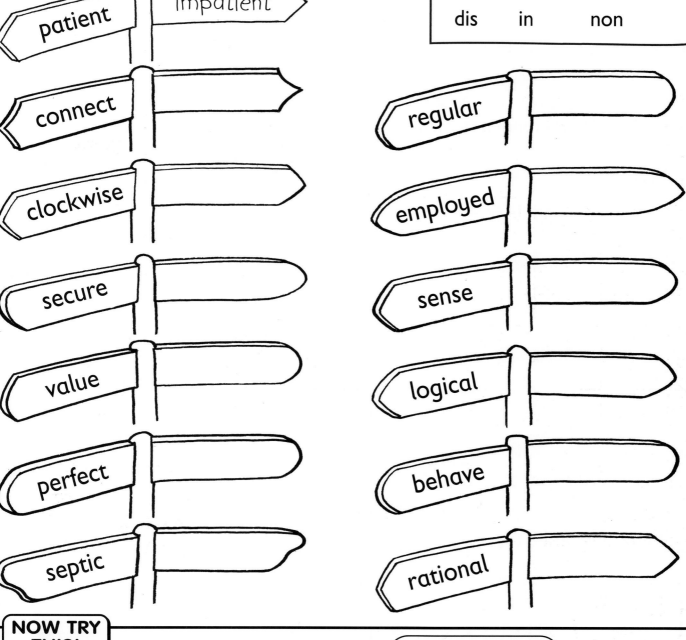

patient — impatient

connect

clockwise

secure

value

perfect

septic

regular

employed

sense

logical

behave

rational

NOW TRY THIS!

- **Write sentences using four words from the signs.**

Think about the types of words that they are.

Teachers' note The children should first read the words on the signs and, if they do not know their meanings, look them up in a dictionary. If they do not know which prefix to use, ask them to try each one orally and to decide which sounds right. This will help them to recall words they have come across in their reading.

100% New Developing Literacy
Word: Structure and Spelling
Ages 8–9
© A & C BLACK

Spelling choice

- **Choose the correct spelling of each word.**
- **Write it in the sentence.**
- **Read the sentence.**

Use a dictionary.

Check the endings of the words.

We went to the _____ to see a pantomime.

theater
theatar
theatre

First the _____ came on stage and told us
about the people in the story.

narratour
narrator
narrater
narratre

Afterwards we took the _____ down to the
shops in the ground floor.

escalator
escalater
escalatre
escalatar

We heard a _____ complaining to the
shop assistant about a dress that had come apart.

customour
customar
customor
customer

Our next door _____ said he saw a woman
stealing a dress while a girl talked to the _____.

neighbor
neighbour
neighber
managre
manager
managar

A police _____ came and arrested her
and handcuffed the _____.

officer
officor
officar
prisoner
prisonour
prisonar

NOW TRY THIS!

- **Complete these words, then write
  a sentence for each one.**

  calib____   massac____   famili____
  smuggl____ conjur____   endeav____

Teachers' note Ask the children to read the sentences with a friend, saying the missing word as
they do so. Ask them to decide which spelling looks right before they check it in a dictionary.

20

100% New Developing Literacy
Word: Structure and Spelling
Ages 8–9
© A & C BLACK

Double or single

- **Read the definitions for the words in the phoneme grids.**
- **Write the missing consonants.**

> The missing consonants could be a single or a double consonant.

Definition	Phoneme grid
An engine	m o _ or
Someone who robs people	r o _ er
Someone who talks a lot	ch a _ er b o x
A red insect with black spots	l a _ y b ir d
Cars, buses, trucks, bikes and so on	t r a _ i c
Loose-fitting	b a _ y
Without a sound	s i _ e n t
A yellow spring flower	d a _ o d i l
A flower with a strong perfume	l i _ y
You take photographs with it	c a _ e r a
A type of hat or part of a car	b o _ e t
Fish that is often canned	t u _ a
Liked by many people	p o _ u l ar
The main city in a country	c a _ i t a l
About, near, at a guess	a _ r o x i m a t e
Exact, right	c o _ e c t

NOW TRY THIS!

- **Practise spelling the words in the phoneme frames.**

Look   Say   Cover   Write   Check

Teachers' note Ask the children to read each clue with a friend, and to say the answer. Ask them to try both a single and a double consonant. Discuss whether these affect the vowel that comes before it, and how. Remind them of their previous learning about doubling consonants in order to give the correct vowel sounds when a suffix is added.

**100% New Developing Literacy
Word: Structure and Spelling
Ages 8–9
© A & C BLACK**

All of an age

- **Add the suffix** `age` **to the word in bold type to make a noun.**
- **Write the new word in the gap.**

> Read the sentences and notice how the two words are used differently.

The farmer said he needed to dig ditches to **drain** the field.	The farmer said he needed to dig ditches in the field for _____.
A tennis ball in a gutter can **block** the drainpipe.	A tennis ball in the gutter can cause a _____ in the drainpipe.
Razia is going to **marry** Imran next month.	The _____ of Razia and Imran will be next month.
A notice in the shop said that you must pay for anything you **break**.	A notice in the shop said that you must pay for any _____.
We paid the removal company to **store** our furniture for six months.	We paid the removal company for the _____ of our furniture for six months.
The shop will charge us to **carry** the fridge from the warehouse to our house.	The shop will charge us for the _____ of the fridge to our house.
We have to pay for the seller to **pack** the goods and to **post** them.	We have to pay the seller for the _____ and _____ of the goods.

NOW TRY THIS!

- **Write three rules for adding** `age` **to a verb to make a noun.**

> Remember you have to change some words before you add `age`.

Teachers' note The children should read the sentences with both forms of the word in order to develop awareness of which is correct. Remind them of their previous learning about changes to a base word when a suffix is added: for example, dropping the final **e** and changing **y** to **i**.

**100% New Developing Literacy
Word: Structure and Spelling
Ages 8–9
© A & C BLACK**

What's my line?

• Play 'What's my line?'

★ You need a partner.

★ Cut out the cards. Place the picture cards face down in one area, and the word cards face down in another.

★ Take turns to turn over a picture card and a word card. Can you add the suffix ‖ist‖ to the word to make a noun for someone who does the action or uses the object in the picture? If you can, write the noun and keep the cards. If you can't, turn the cards over again.

★ The winner is the player with the most new words when all the cards have been used.

art	cycle	cello	cartoon
piano	harp	organ	tour
violin	diary	novel	oboe

NOW TRY THIS!

• **Write three rules for adding ‖ist‖ to a word to make a noun for a person.**

Teachers' note Working in pairs or small groups, the children say the word for each person and then write it, or type it on a computer, noticing whether the spell-checker highlights it as wrong, then using the spell-checker to correct it. They can then discuss how the base word has changed: y changes to i and final vowels are dropped.

100% New Developing Literacy
Word: Structure and Spelling
Ages 8–9
© A & C BLACK

Word factory

- **Choose the word to match each place.**
- **Write the word on the sign.**

> The roots of the words come from Latin words for the objects kept in the places or the activities that happen there.

~~~
Word-bank
~~~

dormitory	laboratory	observatory	refrectory
factory	memory	rectory	territory

Which is the rector's house?

Where do scientists do experiments?

Where can we watch stars and planets?

Where do a group of people sleep?

Where are things manufactured?

Which part of the brain remembers?

Where do a large group of people eat?

What is land ruled by another country?

NOW TRY THIS!

- **Write the words that end in** ⬚ ory ⬚.

1 It is sometimes called a toilet but the root word is from Latin for <u>wash</u>.

    l _ _ _ _ ory

2 We use this word for a glass extension to a house but the root word is from Latin for <u>keep</u> or <u>preserve</u>.

    c _ _ _ _ _ _ _ _ _ ory

Teachers' note Encourage the children to link words from the clues to the words in the word-bank. Point out segments of words and look up their meanings. Introduce synonyms for other words to help them: *watch/observe/observatory*, also Latin words: *terra* (earth), *dormire* (to sleep), *refectio* (food, meal), *laborare* (to work).

100% New Developing Literacy
Word: Structure and Spelling
Ages 8–9
© A & C BLACK

Glossary

- **Find the words that match the definitions.**
- **Write them in the glossary.**
- **Cut out the words and definitions and put them in alphabetical order.**

The root word comes from a Latin word for what happens in the place or what is kept there.

Word-bank

glossary	dictionary	granary	mortuary	diary
library	dispensary	infirmary	statuary	aviary

Glossary

	A book in which the day's events are written
	A place where the bodies of dead people are kept
	Part of a book where important words are listed
	A building where grain is stored
	A building where sick people are cared for
	A book that lists words and their meanings
	A place where medicines are dispensed
	A building or room where books are kept
	A place where statues are kept or displayed
	A place where birds are kept

NOW TRY THIS!

- **What are kept in these?**

apiary   formicary   vespiary

Use a dictionary.

Teachers' note Encourage the children to link words from the clues to those in the word-bank: *dispense/dispensary, grain/granary, statue/statuary*. Point out segments of words, also synonyms: *manufacture/factory, infirm/sick*. Introduce Latin and Greek words (for examples see *Notes on the activities*, pages 7–8).

100% New Developing Literacy
Word: Structure and Spelling
Ages 8–9
© A & C BLACK

Community of words

- ## Make a noun ending in ⬚ty .
- ## Cross out the word in bold type. Write the noun in the gap.

The motorcyclist wore
a crash helmet for **safe**

_____ .

The new shop
advertised in the local
paper for **public**

_____ .

The young
gymnast's **agile**

_____

impressed the judges.

Salim's **able**

_____

to multiply was
remarkable.

Local people
said that the round
house was an **odd**

_____ .

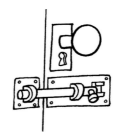

Mum bolted the
door for **secure**

_____ .

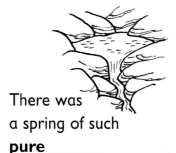

There was
a spring of such
pure _____
that we could drink
its water.

Jock chose Springer
spaniels because of
their great **loyal**

_____ .

We pay for the
amount of **electric**

_____

we use.

There are only two
shops in our **local**

_____ .

Emma's favourite
active

_____

is cycling.

Cara's **special**

_____

was juggling while
standing on one leg.

NOW TRY THIS!

- ## Make ⬚ty nouns from these words.

  stable   poor   jolly

Use a
dictionary.

Teachers' note Ask the children whether the first example sounds right and which word sounds wrong. How can they change that word so that it makes sense? Ask them how they can change _public_ so that it makes sense and, if necessary, introduce the noun _publicity_. Focus on how the base words changes (**i** is added before **ty**).

**100% New Developing Literacy
Word: Structure and Spelling
Ages 8–9
© A & C BLACK**

Word dance

- **Add** `ance` **to the verb to make a noun.**
- **Write the noun on the dancer's banner.**
- **Write instructions for changing the verb.**

annoy

| Just add 'ance'. |

guide

disturb

enter

insure

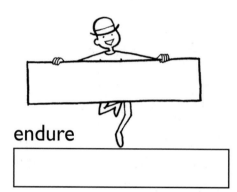

endure

apply

tolerate

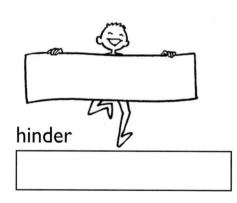

hinder

defy

attend

admit

Teachers' note Give the children sentences using the verb forms of the words and ask what is wrong with them, e.g. *He showed his annoy by frowning; We did not know the way, so we asked for guide; There was a disturb in the street.* Show the children how to convert the verbs into nouns, which make sense here. *Does the base word change when -ance is added*?

**100% New Developing Literacy
Word: Structure and Spelling
Ages 8–9
© A & C BLACK**

Making a difference

- **Write the verb each** ╎ence╎ **noun comes from.**
- **Write an instruction for adding the suffix** ╎ence╎.
- **Say the verb and the noun.**
- **Circle any phonemes that change.**

The festival will **coincide** with the summer fair. What a **coincidence**.

Verb	Noun	Instruction
exist	existence	Just add 'ence'.
	correspondence	
	obedience	
	offence	
	conference	
	pretence	
	preference	
	confidence	
	subsidence	
	residence	
	persistence	
	reference	
	disobedience	
	difference	
	defence	

NOW TRY THIS!

- **Write sentences using four of the** ╎ence╎ **nouns.**
- **Then write four sentences using the verbs they came from.**

Teachers' note Give the children sentences using the verb forms of the words and ask what is wrong with them: for example, *He said, "I can existence on water for ten days"; I correspondence with my pen friend*. Discuss how to identify the verbs the nouns are formed from. *How does adding -ence change the base word – if at all?*

28

100% New Developing Literacy
Word: Structure and Spelling
Ages 8–9
© A & C BLACK

Selective adjectives

- **Match the verbs and the adjectives.**
- **List the adjectives in groups.**
- **Write captions that say how the verb changes when the suffix** `ive` **is added.**

Verbs			
express ✔	attend	act	mass
produce	disrupt	reflect	expand
extend	corrode	create ✔	receive
deceive	narrate	sense	offend
respond	conclude	explode	defend
obstruct	exclude	include	attract

Adjectives			
attractive	defensive	disruptive	attentive
exclusive	expansive	inclusive	extensive
corrosive	conclusive	creative ✔	offensive
sensitive	narrative	massive	receptive
responsive	deceptive	reflective	explosive
obstructive	productive	expressive ✔	

expressive

Just add 'ive'.

creative

NOW TRY THIS!

- **Form adjectives using the suffix** `ive` **from:**

cooperate   explore   capture

Teachers' note Use the completed examples to demonstrate how adjectives work in sentences: for example, *He had an expressive face; The artist was very creative.* Use these to explore how adding **ive** changes the base word, if at all.

100% New Developing Literacy
Word: Structure and Spelling
Ages 8–9
© A & C BLACK

Adjective arithmetic

• **Complete each sum.**

Example:

danger + ous = *dangerous*

The answers are adjectives with the suffix ous .

peril + ous   = _____

poison + ous = _____

pomp + ___   = _____

Just add ous .

fame – e + ous   = _____

nerve – e + ___   = _____

ridicule – ___   = _____

adventure – ___ + ___ = _____

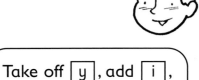
Take off e and add ous .

glory – y + ___   = _____

envy – ___ + ___   = _____

vary – ___ + ___   = _____

fury – ___ + ___   = _____

Take off y , add i , then add ous .

rigour – our + ___ + ___   = _____

glamour – our + ___ + ___ = _____

vigour – ___ + ___ + ___   = _____

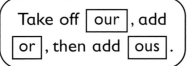
Take off our , add or , then add ous .

NOW TRY THIS!

• **Write sentences using four of the** ous **adjectives.**
• **Then write four sentences using the nouns they came from.**

Teachers' note Remind the children of their previous learning about adding suffixes. Use other examples for practice: (just add **ous**) *coniferous*; (take off **e** then add **ous**) *continuous*; (take off **y**, add **i**, then add **ous**) *furious, harmonious*; (take off **our**, add **or** then add **ous**) *humorous*. There are also some words that drop **e** and take **i** before **ous**: *gracious*.

100% New Developing Literacy
Word: Structure and Spelling
Ages 8–9
© A & C BLACK

That's fantastic!

- **Proofread the story.**
- **Draw a line through the words that should be adjectives.**
- **Add the suffix** `ic` **to make adjectives.**
- **Write these in the margin.**

atomic

Planetto and Stella were flying around in space one day, listening to their space iPods, when they heard a little voice: "I'm Lapinus, an atom rabbit. I'd like to be your pet. It's a base animal right to be a pet."

"Sorry – I'm allergy to animal fur," said Stella. "I can only have robot animals for pets."

"I'm no ordinary rabbit," said Lapinus. "I can change size. One minute I'm microscope and the next I'm giant. I can sing with my melody voice. I am very artist and poet, too."

Stella, a romance girl, took a few flaps towards the little creature but Planetto was less sympathy: "Stella! Don't be idiot. You'll start sneezing any minute and you'll come out in horror spots! Let's have a game of magnet Scrabble instead. I'll give the rabbit a carrot. I brought some nice organ ones that granddad grew in his cosmos allotment."

I suppose so," said Stella. "Which language shall we play in – English, Martian or Arab?"

"May I play?" asked Lapinus. "That would be fantasy!"

NOW TRY THIS!

- **Write sentences using** `ic` **adjectives made from these nouns.**

cube   history   symbol   metal

Teachers' note Use the heading (*fantastic*) to introduce the suffix -ic. Ask the children to read the text aloud with a partner and to listen for words that sound wrong. Ask them to change these words by adding -ic. During the plenary session ask them to say how they changed the base words where necessary, and why.

100% New Developing Literacy
Word: Structure and Spelling
Ages 8–9
© A & C BLACK

Special adjectives

- **Write an adjective ending** cial **or** tial **to replace the words in bold type.**

Use a dictionary.

Example:

| The film star's house is like a **palace**. | | The film star's house is palatial. |

| We learned all about the muscles in the face. | | We learned all about the _____ muscles. |

| There was a file of papers from the office of the council. | | There was a file of _____ council papers. |

| He told me some information in confidence. | | He told me some _____ information. |

| We were soaked by the rain that fell in torrents. | | We were soaked by the _____ rain. |

| My sister is an expert on finance. | | My sister is a _____ expert. |

| Singers and other stars have a lot of influence in fashion. | | Singers and other stars are very _____ in fashion. |

NOW TRY THIS!

- **Make notes about the changes to the spellings of base words when you add** cial **or** tial **.**

Teachers' note Remind the children of the ways of forming adjectives that they know: for example, by adding the suffixes -ive or -ous to base words. Introduce the suffix -ic. Ask the children to read the text aloud with a partner and to listen for words that sound wrong. Ask them to change these words by adding -ic and say how they changed the base words where necessary, and why.

100% New Developing Literacy
Word: Structure and Spelling
Ages 8–9
© A & C BLACK

Hidden a and double ll

- **You can use the suffix ly to form adverbs from adjectives. This page is about adverbs ending ally .**

In words ending ally you do not hear the a sound. *Logically* sounds like *logicly*.

Example: casual → casually

They were dressed in **casual** clothes.

They strolled **casually** through the park.

- **Add the suffix ly to these adjectives.**

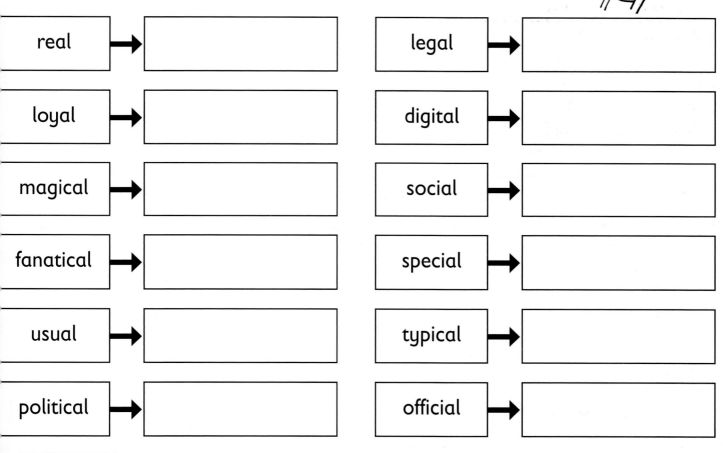

real	→		legal	→	
loyal	→		digital	→	
magical	→		social	→	
fanatical	→		special	→	
usual	→		typical	→	
political	→		official	→	

NOW TRY THIS!

- **Write sentences using these adjectives and the ally adverbs formed from them.**

  equal   technical   ideal

Teachers' note Invite volunteers to come out and write the base words and add -ly. Discuss changes to the base word. Then introduce base words ending -al and read the example with the children. Ask them which letter they do not hear when they say *casually* (in addition to the **u**).

100% New Developing Literacy
Word: Structure and Spelling
Ages 8–9
© A & C BLACK

To double or not to double

- **Use the suffix** ☐ed☐ **to make the past tense of each verb.**
- **Write it in one of the charts.**

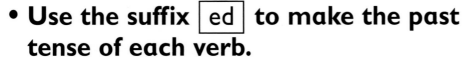

```
ooooooooooooooooooooooooooooooooooooo
```

Verbs

appal	crawl	hail	oil	rival	spoil
appeal	dial	label	pedal	sail	twirl
boil	travel	level	peel	scowl	fool
cancel	fulfil	marvel	propel	seal	bawl
control	haul	nail	reveal	shovel	

Single l		Double l	

- **Complete the rules for past tense verbs ending with l:**

If the **l** follows a single vowel _____

If the **l** follows two vowels _____

If the **l** follows a consonant _____

NOW TRY THIS!

- **Circle the words that are spelt wrongly and write them correctly.**

  bowled   coilled   crawled   failed   fuelled

  instilled   repeled   quarrelled   tunnelled.

Teachers' note Read the first verb in the list and ensure that the children know its meaning (use it in a sentence: *Joe's poor work will appal his parents*). Ask the children to help you to write the sentence in the past tense: *Joe's poor work appalled his parents*). Note the double l.

100% New Developing Literacy
Word: Structure and Spelling
Ages 8–9
© A & C BLACK

Verbifying

- Add ify to turn the nouns into verbs.
- Write the verbs in the sentences.

You might need to change the spellings of the nouns.

beauty   Shona thought the shampoo would _beautify_ her hair.

glory   People sings hymns that _____ God.

mummy   The Egyptians used to _____ the bodies of people who died.

pure   You can _____ water by boiling it.

solid   You can _____ water by freezing it.

terror   A spider would _____ my mum, but not me.

intense   You can _____ the heat of a cooker by turning the knob.

class   We can _____ shapes by the number of sides.

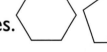

electric   The farmer said he would _____ the fence to keep the cattle in the field.

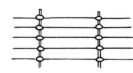

horror   It would _____ me if I saw an animal being treated cruelly.

NOW TRY THIS!

- **Write sentences using the verbs from these nouns.**

  sign   identity   note

Teachers' note Remind the children of the roles of nouns and verbs in sentences, if necessary. Ask them to describe the changes made to the base word *beauty* in order to make *beautify* (take off **y** before adding **-ify**). The children should notice the way in which each noun changes, if at all, when **ify** is added.

100% New Developing Literacy
Word: Structure and Spelling
Ages 8–9
© A & C BLACK

Verb brain

- **Add** ⬜ise⬜ **to the words in bold type.**
- **Write the verbs.**

You might need to change the spellings of the nouns.

Make into **liquid**.

You can *liquidise* fruit to make a drink.

Make **civil**.

_____ used to mean to build cities.

Give a **summary**.

I shall _____ what I have just said.

Add a **motor**.

I want to _____ my roller blades.

Turn into a **fossil**.

Rocks can _____ animals and plants.

Use a **symbol**.

Red can _____ good luck.

Make a **fantasy**.

I _____ about winning a gold medal.

NOW TRY THIS!

- **Write sentences using verbs made from these words.**

victim   custom   colony

Teachers' note Introduce the use of the suffix **-ise** to form verbs from nouns and adjectives. Ask the children to notice which endings of base words change when they form these verbs. During the plenary session, discuss why this is: for example, *summaryise* would be clumsy, as would *fantasyise*.

100% New Developing Literacy Word: Structure and Spelling Ages 8–9 © A & C BLACK

Vowel change

- **Write the missing past tenses.**
- **Circle the letters for the vowel phoneme that changes.**

It helps if you read the sentences aloud.

Example:

Lisa is dr(i)ving a sports car.

Lisa has dr(i)ven a sports car.

I was writing a letter.

I have _____ a letter.

A thief was stealing the bag.

A thief has _____ the bag.

Mrs Dunn was speaking to the class.

Mrs Dunn has _____ to the class.

Firewalkers were treading on hot coals.

Firewalkers have _____ on hot coals.

We were hiding in the shed.

We have _____ in the shed.

Jim was choosing a jacket.

Jim has _____ a jacket.

Two men were weaving the mats.

Two men have _____ the mats.

The dog was biting the boy.

The dog has _____ the boy.

The water was freezing.

The water has _____.

NOW TRY THIS!

- **Write sentences using different past tenses of these words.**

  ride   wake   forgive   rise   mistake

Teachers' note Remind the children about the suffix **-en** for changing verbs to form different tenses and use the introductory example to highlight the changes this can make to the main vowel phoneme. Also ask them about the base word for *driving* (*drive*) and invite them to contribute to a set of rules for any changes to the spelling of a base word.

100% New Developing Literacy Word: Structure and Spelling Ages 8–9 © A & C BLACK

Spot the mistake ee

breifly	please	indeed	peeple
cheaply	energee	defeat	feeture
leeking	speedway	treecle	chief
anteaque	procede	batterie	apologey
abbey	personally	releaf	mystyrious
deceive	weekend	reveel	easel
freazing	leegue	magazine	succede
theif	beacon	creeking	believe

Teachers' note Ask the children to correct any /ee/ words they think are wrong. Remind them of the different rules for writing the /ee/ phoneme. They can then cut out the word cards and sort them according to the spelling of the /ee/ phoneme. During the plenary session they could compare their results with those of others and check them using a dictionary.

**100% New Developing Literacy
Word: Structure and Spelling
Ages 8–9
© A & C BLACK**

Not [ay]

- **Write words to match the definitions.**
- **Cut out the words and definitions and put them in alphabetical order for a dictionary of [ain] words.**

All the words end with [ain] that sounds like [in] or [un].

Use a dictionary.

Word-bank

bargain	certain	chieftain	fountain	porcelain
captain	chaplain	curtain	mountain	villain

✂ -

	A very high hill
	Cloth hung at a window
	Sure
	A water feature found in gardens and public places
	The person in charge of a ship
	A good buy; good value for money
	A criminal or bad person
	A priest, imam or other faith leader at a hospital, prison
	The leader of a tribe
	Very delicate china

NOW TRY THIS!

- **Write sentences using five of the words on this page.**

Teachers' note Write up **ai** and ask the children which phoneme it usually spells. Ask them to read the words in the word-bank aloud and then to say what they notice about **ai** in these words (it is pronounced **i** or **uh**).

100% New Developing Literacy
Word: Structure and Spelling
Ages 8–9
© A & C BLACK

• **Write the words with** 2 **in full.**

Hi Rosie. Going 2 the fair 2day with Gemma + her mum + dad + 2 brothers. xx Jane

_____

_____

_____

Hi Sam. Sorry. Got your message 2 late. It 2k ages 2 find my phone. See you 2morrow. Ben

_____

_____

_____

Anna. Please bring your 2lbox 2night. Have 2 fix a broken s2l. Jenny

_____

_____

_____

Hi Ella. Sweet shop has 2 many fruit bars. Selling at 2 pence each. 2 good 2 miss!

_____

_____

_____

Jason. Dad said I can have pet bird: a 2can or cocka2. Have 2 pay £10 2wards it and promise 2 look after it. Cheers, Leroy

_____

_____

_____

Salim – Andy 2k my bike home. Will you ask him 2 keep it until Monday? I've got 2thache. Going 2 dentist. See you, Liam

_____

_____

_____

NOW TRY THIS!

• **Write these words in full.**

2mb   car2nist   s2ping   tat2

Teachers' note Ask the children about the different graphemes that can be used for the /oo/ phoneme and discuss how mobile phone spelling can be useful if they are not sure which is correct. Tell them that they are going to 'translate' words containing 2 in some mobile phone messages into correct spellings.

100% New Developing Literacy Word: Structure and Spelling Ages 8–9
© A & C BLACK

Mobile phone spellings 4 U

• **Write the words with** $\boxed{4}$ **in full.**

Mum
Don't 4get it's Jake's 4th birthday in a 4tnight.
Look 4ward to making the party food. Love Meera

_____
_____
_____
_____

Hi Lee. Sorry – can't af4d to go to the match. It costs a 4tune and Mum has to pay 4 my new school uni4m. Simon

_____
_____
_____
_____

Deepak. I got 4ty plastic 4ks 4 the picnic. The pack broke so I hope none will 4l out. I'll bring them be4 the weekend. Ella

_____
_____
_____
_____

Asma. Weather 4cast looks brilliant 4 your trip to see the water4ll but there will be a heavy rain4ll next week. See you, May

_____
_____
_____
_____

Dad. City's new centre 4ward did a brilliant 4head header last week so I hope they play in the same 4mation again. William

_____
_____
_____
_____

Sean. Don't worry. No one can 4ce you to per4m in the play. See you at the station in the morning – plat4m 4. Cheers, Kyle

_____
_____
_____
_____

NOW TRY THIS!

• **Write sentences with these words in full.**

in4mation	4head	down4l
rein4rce	4giveness	4m

Teachers' note Ask the children about the different graphemes that can be used for the /or/ phoneme and discuss how '4' is a useful abbreviation in mobile phone spelling. Tell them that they are going to 'translate' words containing 4 in some mobile phone messages into correct spellings.

100% New Developing Literacy
Word: Structure and Spelling
Ages 8–9
© A & C BLACK

Gr8 mobile phone spellings

• **Write the words with** 8 **in full.**

Dad. Mum said it's OK to go to the sk8 park with you. I'll w8 for you at the school g8.
Love Sonia

_____

_____

_____

Hi Harry. I'll be l8 for school. There's a big cr8er in High Street so we had to go all the way round Sl8r Street. See you l8r. Luke

_____

_____

_____

Misha. W8r at Fast Food Stop dropped pl8 of pot8oes on Mum's jumper! I'll send you an upd8 l8r. Amy

_____

_____

_____

Calum. Fire in Frock Shop! Started in cr8 under escal8or. Whole street evacu8d. Have to w8 for the all clear. Connor

_____

_____

_____

Connor. The fair's gr8. Just had portr8 done as a heavyw8 boxer! Rosie had hers done as a w8ress. See you. Kevin

_____

_____

_____

Hi Katie. We're at the zoo. A keeper demonstr8d how to look after allig8ors. We're going str8 on to Disneyworld. Love Emma

_____

_____

_____

NOW TRY THIS!

• **Write sentences with these words in full.**

navig8   equ8or   cre8

circul8ing   fr8   rot8ed

Teachers' note Ask the children about the different graphemes that can be used for the /ai/ phoneme and discuss how mobile phone spelling can be useful if they are not sure which is correct. Tell them that they are going to 'translate' words containing 8 in some mobile phone messages into correct spellings.

100% New Developing Literacy Word: Structure and Spelling Ages 8–9 © A & C BLACK

Number plate spellings

- **Read the clues for the words.**
- **Write the missing letters.**

The past tense of bring.

BR_O_U_GHT

Very bad.

DR___DFUL

Kill.

M_RD_R

Sweet, sticky stuff.

TR___CL_

Wider.

BR___D_R

Cake with a hole.

D_____N_T

Sledge.

SL_____

Skin damage from a knock.

BR___S_

Gentle wind.

BR___Z_

Wrinkle.

CR___SE

Stooping.

CR___CH_NG

Bother.

TR___BLE

NOW TRY THIS!

- **Fill in the gaps to make words.**

app___r_nce   c___r_g___s   pl___s_nt

Teachers' note First point out that each dash represents a letter. After they have completed the activity encourage them to compare their answers and their trial attempts with those of a friend, and to discuss how they chose the one they thought was correct. They could then use a dictionary to check them.

100% New Developing Literacy
Word: Structure and Spelling
Ages 8–9
© A & C BLACK

Homophone hints

• Circle the correct words.

> The clues will help you to check the spellings.

> Allow me to help.

We took turns to read
allowed/aloud to the class.

> There is a high mountain nearby.

We are going
to hire/higher a
caravan for our holiday.

> Armies fight battles.

The two armies fought/fort
at the fougth/fort.

> What did you see?

The first seen/scene of
the play was set in a cave.

> To bawl is to shout.

My grandad is
going bald/bawled.

> It was a misty day.

We mist/missed the bus.

> A peddler walks about selling goods.

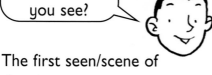

The pedals/peddles
on my bike are red.

> Let's wring the washing.

I rung/wrung the
water out of the dishcloth.

> They went down a coal mine.

The men
mined/mind for coal.

> A guest was ringing the bell.

I guessed/guest
who was at the door.

> She gave a sigh and went outside.

The teacher
sighed/side as she
looked at the messy work.

> She threw a ball to the corgi.

The queen sat on
her throne/thrown.

> **NOW TRY THIS!**

• Write sentences using these homophones.

weather   whether   cereal   serial

check   cheque   flower   flour

Teachers' note Read the sentence to the children, replacing *allowed/aloud* with *let* and ask if it makes sense. Point out that the spelling in the clue shows where one of the words comes from and might not be the correct one in the sentence.

**100% New Developing Literacy
Word: Structure and Spelling
Ages 8–9
© A & C BLACK**

44

In and out

- **Decide which words in the word-bank can have** `in` **as a prefix.**
- **Decide which words can have** `out` **as a prefix.**
- **Write the new words on the Venn diagram.**

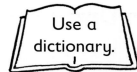

Use a dictionary.

Word-bank

break	~~come~~	going	let	mate	sole
building	dated	grow	line	put	spoken
cast	doors	land	look	side	wit

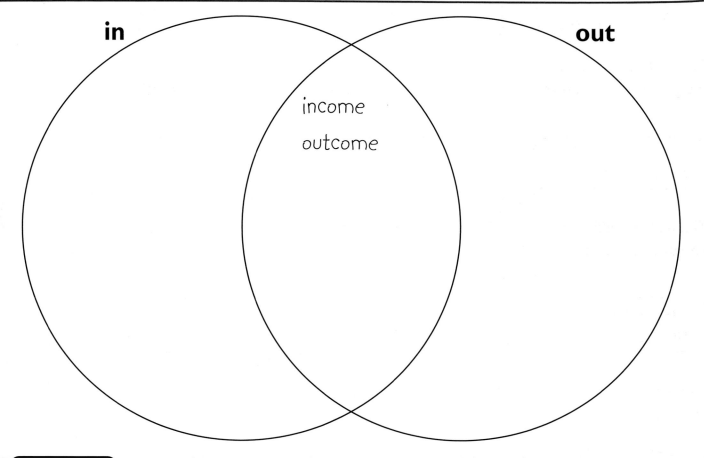

in   **out**

income

outcome

NOW TRY THIS!

- **Choose three words that can have either** `in` **or** `out` **as a prefix.**
- **Write their meanings.**

Teachers' note Use the completed examples to demonstrate that some words can be prefixed by either in- or out-. Use either *building* or *cast* as an example of a word that only makes sense with one of the prefixes. Ask the children whether the prefix **in-** always gives the opposite meaning to the prefix **out-**.

100% New Developing Literacy
Word: Structure and Spelling
Ages 8–9
© A & C BLACK

Up and down

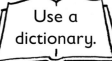
Use a dictionary.

- **Decide which words in the word-bank can have** | up | **as a prefix.**
- **Decide which words can have** | down | **as a prefix.**
- **Write the new words on the Venn diagram.**

Word-bank

~~bringing~~	fall	hill	market	root	surge
cast	keep	lift	rising	side	trodden
date	grade	load	roar	standing	turn

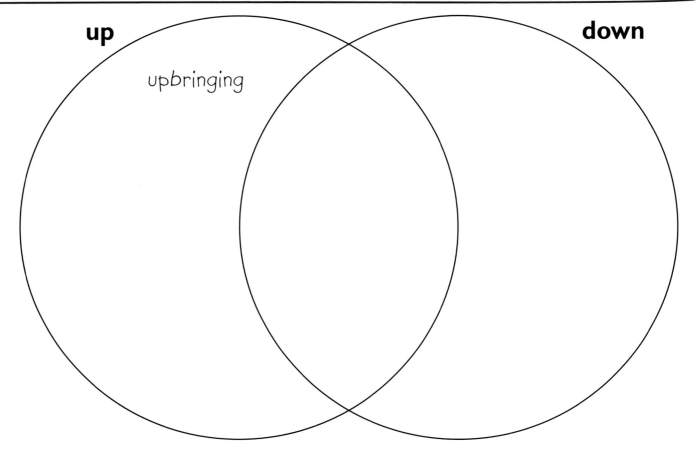

up   **down**

upbringing

NOW TRY THIS!

- **Choose three words that can have either** | up | **or** | down | **as a prefix.**
- **Write their meanings.**

Teachers' note Use the completed example to demonstrate that some words can be prefixed by either **up**- or **down**- and ask why *bringing* would not make sense with **down**- as a prefix. Use *bringing* as an example of a word that only makes sense with **up**- and discuss why. Use *hill* as an example of a word with which either prefix makes sense.

**100% New Developing Literacy
Word: Structure and Spelling
Ages 8–9**
© A & C BLACK

Under or over

- **Write the meaning of each** `over` **word.**

Can you change the prefix `over` **to** `under` **to make a new word?** ✔ **or** ✗

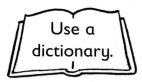

Use a dictionary.

- **Write these new words in the** `under` **glossary.**
- **Write their meanings.**

over words		
overall	A garment worn over all other clothes to protect them	✗
overbalance		
overboard		
overcharge		
overcoat		
overcome		
overripe		
oversleep		
overturn		
overweight		

under words	

NOW TRY THIS!

- **Add the prefix** `under` **or** `over` **to these words to make new words.**
- **Write their meanings.**

  dog   foot   ground   take   water

Teachers' note Read the first example with the children and ask them if all could have the prefix *under* – is *underall* a real word? Look for a base word which makes sense with either *under* or *over*: e.g. *coat*. After writing *undercoat* in the second chart, discuss and enter its meaning, noting that *under* or *over* do not necessarily create words with opposite meanings.

100% New Developing Literacy
Word: Structure and Spelling
Ages 8–9
© A & C BLACK

Word-bites

- **Draw lines to link two word-bites to make new words.**
- **Write the new words on the notepad.**

Use a dictionary.

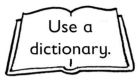

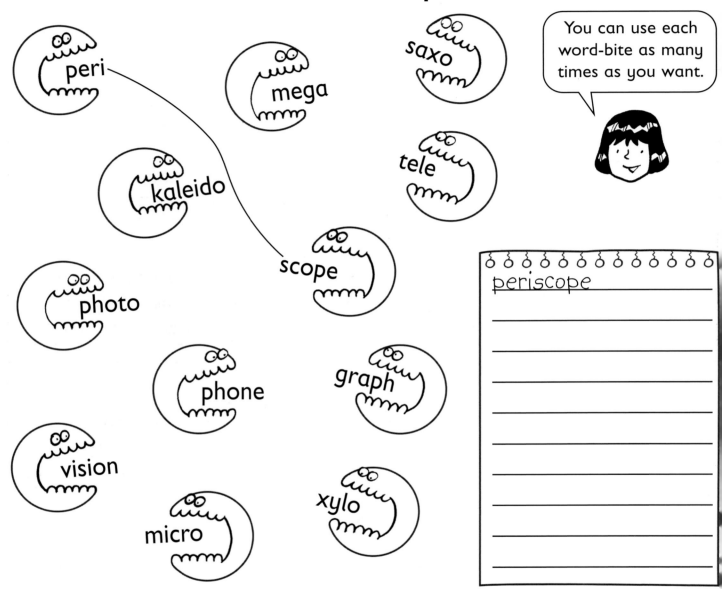

You can use each word-bite as many times as you want.

peri

mega

saxo

kaleido

tele

scope

photo

phone

graph

vision

micro

xylo

periscope

NOW TRY THIS!

- **Write the meanings of six of the new words.**
- **Tell a friend what you think each word-bite means.**

The word-bites come from Latin and Greek.

Teachers' note Explain that these have been called word-bites because they are parts of words that do not seem to be real words, unlike *over* and *all* in *overall*, *down* or *grade* in *downgrade*. Tell the children that these 'word-bites' have meanings but that they come from Latin or Greek.

48

**100% New Developing Literacy
Word: Structure and Spelling
Ages 8–9**
© A & C BLACK

Word-core

- **Make words that contain** `spect` **.**
- **Write the words above their definitions.**

Use a dictionary.

To look into closely

Someone who watches an event

A view of something

A view from a high position

People wear these to help them to see clearly

To look up to

A showy event

Someone the police think might have committed a crime

A rainbow of coloured light that white light splits into

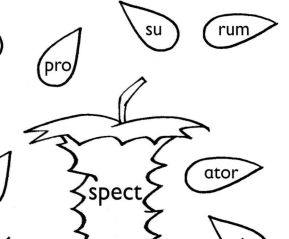

acle su rum pro a ator in re acular ator acles

spect

Amazing and wonderful

NOW TRY THIS!

- **Write a word for a ghost that contains** `spect` **.**
- **Look it up in a dictionary and an etymological dictionary.**
- **Tell a friend how its meaning is linked with the** `spect` **words you made.**

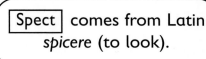

`Spect` comes from Latin *spicere* (to look).

Teachers' note Tell the children that *spect* has been described here as a 'word-core' because it is the core (base) of many words – at the beginning, middle or end of the word. Ask for examples and write these up or display them on an interactive whiteboard, where they can be left to assist the children in completing the page (see *Notes on the activities* page 9).

100% New Developing Literacy
Word: Structure and Spelling
Ages 8–9
© A & C BLACK

Word petals

- **Make a word that matches each definition.**
- **Write the words on the plant pot.**

You might need to change the spellings of the base words.

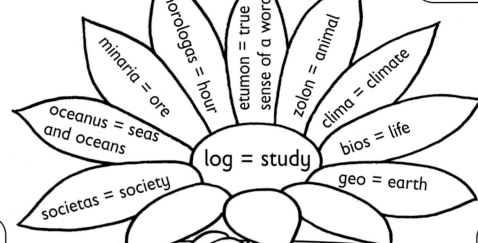

Petals:
- minaria = ore
- horologas = hour
- etumon = true sense of a word
- zolon = animal
- oceanus = seas and oceans
- clima = climate
- bios = life
- societas = society
- geo = earth
- log = study

Some of the words are Greek.

Some of the words are Latin.

1 Study of word meanings _____

2 Study of animals _____

3 Study of society _____

4 Study of time _____

5 Study of climates _____

6 Study of the Earth _____

7 Study of minerals _____

8 Study of oceans _____

9 Study of life _____

NOW TRY THIS!

- **Write words ending in** ⬚ ology ⬚ **that mean:**

  1 The study of stars and planets

  2 The study of history mainly through excavation

- **Use suffixes to make words for people who do these activities.**

Teachers' note Tell the children that **-logy** is a suffix that comes from Greek and ask them for some examples. Ask what kinds of words end with **-logy**. Point out that **-logy** is used in English with bits of words that might come from either Greek or Latin. Tell them that many words connected with sciences or learning come from Latin, Greek or Arabic.

100% New Developing Literacy
Word: Structure and Spelling
Ages 8–9
© A & C BLACK

Compound pairs

- **Make two new words by putting the same word before the words in the pair.**

Example:

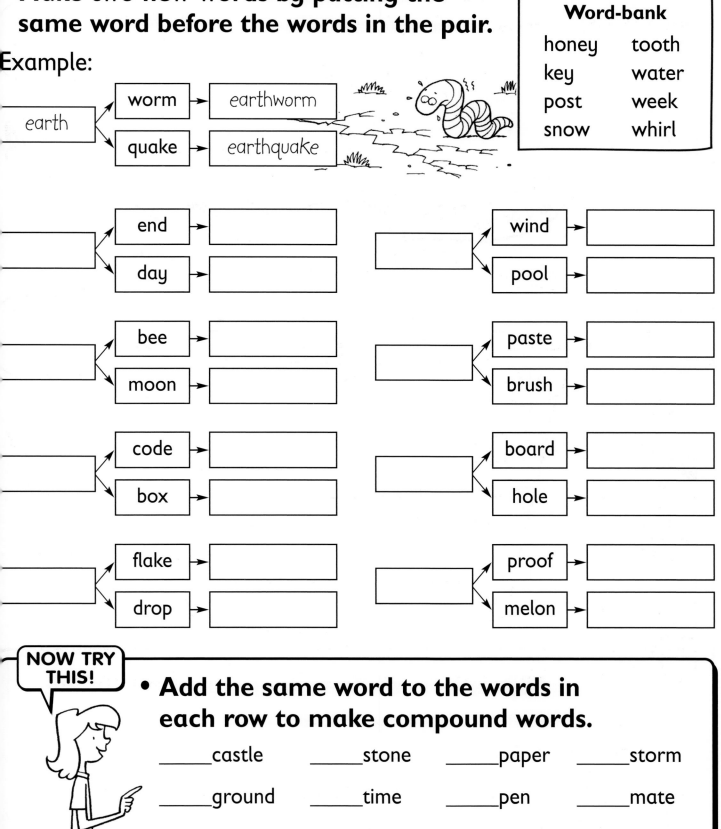

earth → worm → earthworm

earth → quake → earthquake

| | → end → | |
| → day → | |

| | → wind → | |
| → pool → | |

| | → bee → | |
| → moon → | |

| | → paste → | |
| → brush → | |

| | → code → | |
| → box → | |

| | → board → | |
| → hole → | |

| | → flake → | |
| → drop → | |

| | → proof → | |
| → melon → | |

NOW TRY THIS!

- **Add the same word to the words in each row to make compound words.**

_____castle   _____stone   _____paper   _____storm

_____ground   _____time   _____pen   _____mate

Teachers' note Use the introductory example to demonstrate the different ways in which pairs of words can be combined to form compound words. Show the children how to approach the task by 'thinking aloud'.

**100% New Developing Literacy
Word: Structure and Spelling
Ages 8–9
© A & C BLACK**

Prefix it

- **Add prefixes to the word segments to make words with opposite meanings.**
- **Write the words and their meanings.**

inhale
To breathe in

exhale
To breathe out

___port

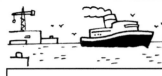

___port

___scend

___scend

___structive

___structive

___flate

___flate

___clude

___clude

NOW TRY THIS!

- **Write pairs of words to make opposites with these meanings.**

_____ Another adjective meaning <u>inside</u>.

_____ Another adjective meaning <u>outside</u>.

_____ To make a car speed up.

_____ To make a car slow down.

Use prefixes from the list. The words must have the same middle segment.

Teachers' note Explain that the pictures and clues are for pairs of words with opposite meanings: for example, *inhale* and *exhale*. Ask what the prefixes **in-** and **ex-** mean here. For the second pair of words, remind the children that the prefixes **in-** and **im-** can have the same meaning but that each is used with base words beginning with particular letters.

**100% New Developing Literacy
Word: Structure and Spelling
Ages 8–9
© A & C BLACK**

Number prefixes

- **Discuss the pictures and captions with a friend.**
  Write the meanings of the prefixes in the Number prefix glossary.

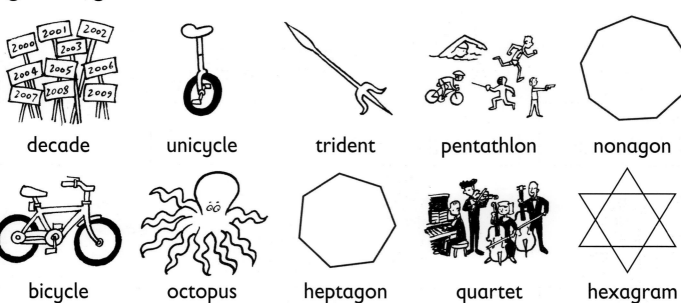

decade   unicycle   trident   pentathlon   nonagon

bicycle   octopus   heptagon   quartet   hexagram

Number prefix glossary			
Prefix	**Meaning**	**Prefix**	**Meaning**
bi		oct	
dec		pent	
hept		quart	
hex		tri	
non		uni	

NOW TRY THIS!

- **Write other words that have these prefixes.**

uni _____   bi _____

tri _____   quart_____

pent _____   hex _____

hept _____   oct _____

non _____   dec _____

Teachers' note This could be introduced through the children's knowledge of shapes: for example, *triangle*, *quadrilateral*, *pentagon*. Which part of the word tells them how many sides the shape has and help them to link this with other words with that prefix: e.g. *tricycle*, *quad-bike*, *pentathlon*. Tell them that the number prefixes come from Latin and Greek words for those numbers.

100% New Developing Literacy
Word: Structure and Spelling
Ages 8–9
© A & C BLACK

Word spiders

- Split the words into segments that can be parts of other words.
- Make new words with the segments.
- Each word must link to another with the same segment.
- Continue the spidergram.

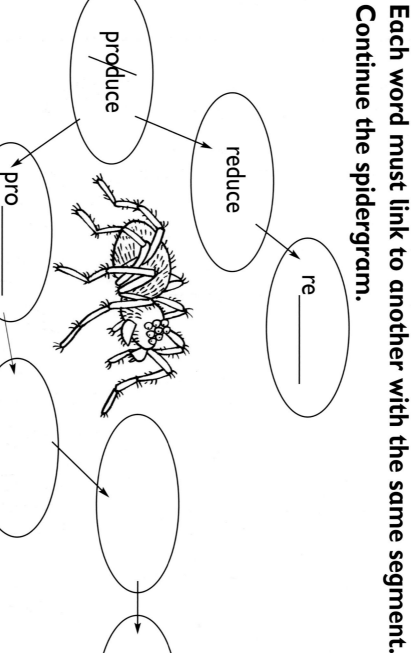

NOW TRY THIS!

- Start a new spidergram with a different word.

Teachers' note Remind the children that some segments of words can be found in several other words and that there is often a linked meaning: for example, *produce/reduce*, also *produce/product/proceed* and *reduce/release*. The children's task is to make a web of words with links.

100% New Developing Literacy
Word: Structure and Spelling
Ages 8–9
© A & C BLACK

A base to build on

- Add different prefixes and suffixes to each base to make different words. You can add more than one suffix.

You might need to change the spelling of the base.

ject

dejected

vert

suit

tend

vict

NOW TRY THIS!

- **Tell a friend how these bases are alike.**

struct   stroy   join   junct

Teachers' note Remind the children that some segments of words can be found in several other words and that there is often a linked meaning: e.g *dejected/subject/inject/injection/injected/ reject/rejected/rejection/object/objection/objected.*

100% New Developing Literacy Word: Structure and Spelling Ages 8–9 © A & C BLACK

55

Word changer

- **Change one segment of the word to make a new word.**
- **Keep changing a segment until you reach the end of the row.**
- **Read each word aloud.**

A segment of a word has a meaning. It can be a base, a prefix or a suffix.

de/flect	Ł	re/flect	Ł	re/ply	Ł	ap/ply
be/side	Ł		Ł		Ł	
ex/ist	Ł		Ł		Ł	
en/able	Ł		Ł		Ł	
ex/port	Ł		Ł		Ł	
un/do	Ł		Ł		Ł	

 NOW TRY THIS!

- **Choose six words from this page.**
- **Add another segment to each word like this:**

de/flect/ion   un/do/ing   ex/ist/ence

Teachers' note Remind the children that some segments of words, including prefixes and suffixes, can be found in several other words and that there is often a linked meaning, which might not be clear if the segments come from other languages: for example, *flect* comes from *flectere* (Latin, bend).

100% New Developing Literacy Word: Structure and Spelling Ages 8–9 © A & C BLACK

- **Listen to the words.**
- **Write the missing letters.**
- **After you have written all the words, write another** [tu] **word using the same base.**

When you hear [chew] in a word that has nothing to do with chewing it is usually spelled [tu].

Word	New word	Word	New word
1 actual	actually	10	
2		11	
3		12	
4		13	
5		14	
6		15	
7		16	
8		17	
9		18	

NOW TRY THIS!

- **Write six other words with the** [chew] **sound:**

multi_ _ _ _   _ _tor   vir_ _ _

atti_ _ _ _   cos_ _ _ _

✂ -

1 actual	2 spiritual	3 tune	4 fortune	5 congratulate	6 institute
7 eventual	8 tube	9 habitual	10 perpetual	11 tuba	12 situate
13 spiritual	14 spatula	15 statue	16 student	17 stupid	18 substitute

Teachers' note Cut off the bottom strip first, then read the words aloud for the children to spell. Use the completed example and others not in the word list to remind the children of the spelling of the 'chew' sound in most words. Ask them to listen carefully and write the letters for every phoneme. It will help if you enunciate very clearly.

100% New Developing Literacy
Word: Structure and Spelling
Ages 8–9
© A & C BLACK

In the queue

- Circle the spelling mistakes.
- Write the words correctly in the margin.

	If something is cirqular it is the shape of a circle.
	The opposite of masquline is feminine.
	If events happen consequtively they happen one after the other.
	We queued up for kebabs at the barbeque while Dad was slicing a qucumber for the salad.
	My exquse for getting the wrong answer was that I had lost my calqulator.
	To make an electrical cirquit you need a metal pathway of wire and other metal things without any breaks but do not connect it to the mains because you could be electroquted.
	The police officer aqused the man of stealing the purse and he was prosequted.
	A qube has six square sides but another shape with two square sides and four rectangular sides is called a quboid.
	I clicked on File and Open to read a doqument on my computer but one partiqular file would not open.
	People were evaquated from their homes during the flood; it was miraqulous that no one was drowned.

NOW TRY THIS!

- **Write words with** | cu | **that mean:**

an instrument with two eyepieces for looking at distant objects: bin_ _ _ _ _ _ _ _

a disease of the lungs: tub_ _ _ _ _osis

very strange: pe_ _ _iar

a prickly animal: po_ _ _ _ine

injection to prevent disease: ino_ _ _ _ _ion

Teachers' note Use the page heading to demonstrate the spelling of a word in which the **c** and **oo** phonemes are spelled **qu** and **eue**. Then remind the children of the **c** and **u** spellings of the same phonemes. They should look carefully at each **qu** they see in the sentences and correct it if necessary.

100% New Developing Literacy
Word: Structure and Spelling
Ages 8–9
© A & C BLACK

Word segments

- **Split the words into segments that have a meaning.**

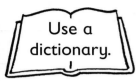
Use a dictionary.

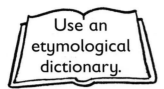
Use an etymological dictionary.

If the segments come from another language, you might be able to work out what they mean from other words that contain them.

- **Write each segment on a segment of an orange.**
- **Label the segments:** prefix , base , suffix .

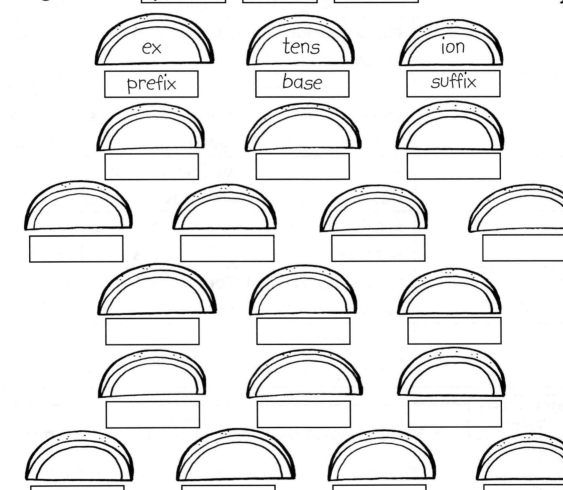

extension — ex (prefix), tens (base), ion (suffix)

disgusted

unexpected

reappearing

overbalanced

expensively

NOW TRY THIS!

- **Choose four words from this page.**
- **Write the meaning of each segment.**

Teachers' note The children's task is to identify word segments that have meaning – sometimes this is easier to identify if other words with similar segments are considered: e.g. *pens/pense* occurs in *compensate, dispense, expense, suspense*.

**100% New Developing Literacy
Word: Structure and Spelling**
Ages 8–9
© A & C BLACK

Help words

- **Read the words.**
- **Circle the tricky part.**
- **Choose a word that will help you to spell it.**
- **Tell a friend how this word will help.**

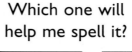

Which one will help me spell it?

Help words

compete
define
familiar
historic
ignore
know
librarian
similarity
torrential
type

family	definite
Help word	Help word
_____	_____

library	typical
Help word	Help word
_____	_____

ignorant ignorance	knowledge	similar
Help word	Help word	Help word
_____	_____	_____

competition	history	torrent
Help word	Help word	Help word
_____	_____	_____

NOW TRY THIS!

- **Choose three words from the boxes.**
- **Write sentences using these words.**

What shall I write?

Teachers' note Show the children how words from the same root as a tricky word can help with its spelling because of changes to phonemes: for example, the **i** in *family* is often missed out because it is unstressed, but the same letter in *familiar* represents the /i/ phoneme.

100% New Developing Literacy Word: Structure and Spelling Ages 8–9 © A & C BLACK

Help sentences

- **Complete the sentences to help you to spell tricky words.**
- **Tell a friend how the sentence helps.**

Example:

The architect designed an <u>arch</u>.

Clue:

There is _____ in my sandwiches.

Clue:

__ am on a cruise.

Clue:

I cut a piece of _____.

Clue:

There is a _____ and a _____ in the cupboard.

Clue:

Clue:

A stomach is like a _____.

The shepherd _____ sheep.

Clue:

NOW TRY THIS!

- **Write helpful sentences for spelling these words.**

  bruise   biscuit   niece   government

Teachers' note Point out the first example (*architect*) and ask the children what is difficult about spelling this word and how the sentence helps. Notice that *architect* has **ch** for the /c/ phoneme and that *arch*, the first part of the word, has **ch** for the /ch/ phoneme when it is a word in its own right. (However, the two words come from different roots.)

**100% New Developing Literacy
Word: Structure and Spelling
Ages 8–9
© A & C BLACK**

Word stories

- **Read the clue.**
- **Write the answer.**
- **Explain how the clue helps you to spell the word.**

| This day of the week is named after the Norse god Woden. | _____ |

| This word for a long time without rain comes from Old English drugað* (dry). | _____ |

| <u>Kerchief</u> is an old word for a small scarf tied around the neck. | _____ |

| This word for a royal rule comes from the Latin word <u>regnum</u> (rule). | _____ |

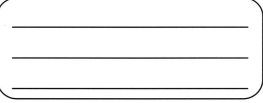

| This word for a boat comes from Dutch <u>jacht</u>. | _____ |

* ð is pronounced like th in the .

NOW TRY THIS!

- **Write the stories of these words.**

guilty   journey   sword   woman

How shall I begin?

Teachers' note Explain that many English words come from other languages and that these roots sometimes give rise to unexpected spellings. Provide etymological dictionaries so that the children can look up the histories of the words. This is a good opportunity for encouraging an interest in word roots and in other languages.

**100% New Developing Literacy
Word: Structure and Spelling
Ages 8–9**
© A & C BLACK

New words

- **Try to read the difficult words in bold type.**
- **See if you can figure out what they mean.**
- **Read them aloud with a friend.**
- **Write their meanings.**

Think about...

... different spellings of phonemes...

... prefixes you know...

... suffixes you know...

... the sense of the word in the sentence...

... other parts of words you know...

Word and sentence	Meaning
I shall **accompany** Phil to the club.	
The village held its **biennial** festival this week. VILLAGE FÊTE	
The old house had **castellated** walls.	
The teacher praised Simon for his **conscientiousness** in class.	
Some villages were **depopulated** when the old lead mines closed.	
We bought a couple of odd chairs that were not too **dissimilar**.	
Mr Rose said he would like a **facsimile** of the document.	
The old book had a lovely **frontispiece** with a picture of a garden.	

NOW TRY THIS!

- **Choose one of the words above.**
- **Draw some 'thought bubbles' and write in them how you figured out how to read it.**
- **Draw some more 'thought bubbles' and write in them how you figured out its meaning.**

eachers' note Read the introduction with the children and emphasise that they can use ideas such s these to help them to read, understand and spell difficult words they come across without the eed for a dictionary.

100% New Developing Literacy
Word: Structure and Spelling
Ages 8–9
© A & C BLACK

Great ideas

- **What makes these words difficult to spell?**
- **Circle the tricky part and write your 'great idea' to help you to spell the word.**

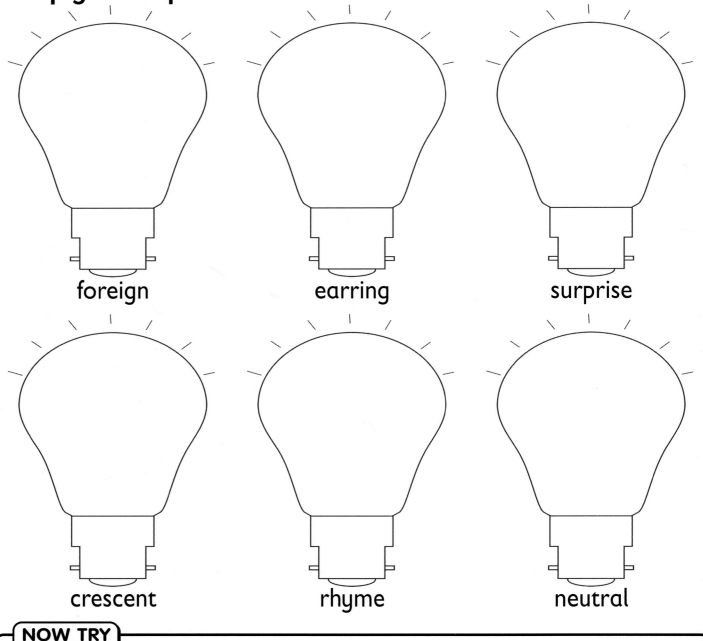

foreign

earring

surprise

crescent

rhyme

neutral

NOW TRY THIS!

- **List six other words you have found difficult to spell.**
- **Circle the tricky parts and write your 'great ideas'.**

Hmmm… let's see…

Teachers' note It is useful if the children have first completed page 63. Remind them of the tips provided on that page for reading, understanding and spelling difficult words. Here their task is to spot the tricky parts of familiar words and to develop their own strategies for spelling them.

100% New Developing Literacy Word: Structure and Spelling Ages 8–9
© A & C BLACK